MW00364423

# OUR
# BUCKET
# LIST
## ADVENTURES

KORIE HEROLD | Paige Tate & Co

# Paige Tate & Co.

*Our Bucket List Adventures*
*Copyright © Korie Herold*

*Published in 2023 by Blue Star Press*
*Paige Tate & Co. is an imprint of Blue Star Press*
*PO Box 8835, Bend, OR 97708*
*contact@paigetate.com | www.paigetate.com*

*Illustrations and Design by Korie Herold*

*ISBN: 9781950968831*
*Printed in Colombia*

*10 9 8 7 6 5 4 3 2*

*This bucket list belongs to :*

_____

_____

_____

_____

*Date :* _____

# INTRODUCTION

If you're reading this, I must assume you and your significant other are motivated to accomplish your goals together, and want a place to get started.

The journal in your hands isn't just for the thrill seekers, as most bucket lists seem to be. This journal is for the goal setters. The doers. The couples who like to make things happen, both big and small.

This journal is for any couple who wants to accomplish a goal, and be able to look back on their shared experience in a tangible way. Not only that, but be able to cherish a book of "life highlights," if you will, for decades to come.

This journal provides space to document bucket list items in a brief format (one page), or in a longer format (two pages). You two decide which items from your list need more room to document.

To use this journal, start by making a list of all the things you and your significant other have ever wanted to do. We've provided space to write them down on the next page. Once you have your list, you can decide which items you want to put on a long format, or a brief format page. Be sure to add your bucket list items to the index provided in the back, and note which numbers correlate to each goal. This way, you can find exactly what you're looking for to continue filling out your journal.

The two page format entries were created with space for photos. A single 3"x 5" photo or two 2"x 3" photo stickers fit great. Or, you can use the space for other forms of proof you completed the goal, like ticket stubs, maps, or postcards. If you find yourself running out of room, there are additional pages in the back for you to store mementos from your adventures.

Tip: Photo stickers work great in this journal. You can have your photos printed onto stickers through various online printers, or you can purchase a portable photo sticker printer to use. It's not necessary by any means, but rather a recommendation to consider.

Additionally, there is a sheet of gold stars in the back of this journal. Who doesn't love getting a gold star?! I was most certainly that kid. As you accomplish items off your bucket list, add a star to the entry page of the completed goal. Over time, you'll be able to flip through the journal and see just how many of your goals you've accomplished together! Also, there are plenty of extra stars included; sometimes you just need to give yourself a gold star for getting through the day, and I'm here to help with that.

So, go ahead. You have full permission to dream big and start doing all the things you've always wanted to do. Get to it!

Onward and Upward,
Korie Herold

I would love to see *Our Bucket List Adventures* in your hands, conquering those bucket list items. Use #ourbucketlistBOOK and tag @korieherold to connect on social media.

# BUCKET LIST IDEAS
## TO INSPIRE AND MOTIVATE

Sometimes you just need a place to start, or some fresh ideas that
resonate with you. Here are a few ideas worthy of any couple's bucket list.

## SMALL IDEAS

ORGANIZE A BOOK CLUB
TAKE A COOKING CLASS
BEFRIEND ANOTHER COUPLE
BAKE A CAKE FROM SCRATCH
HOST A DINNER PARTY
GROW A GARDEN
LEARN A NEW SKILL/CRAFT TOGETHER
VISIT A MUSEUM YOU'VE NEVER BEEN TO
COMPLETE AN INTRICATE JIGSAW PUZZLE
BE A VEGETARIAN/VEGAN FOR A WEEK
GET TO KNOW YOUR NEIGHBORS
VISIT ALL YOUR LOCAL PARKS
TAKE DANCE CLASSES
VOLUNTEER FOR A CAMPAIGN
WRITE YOUR OWN MURDER MYSTERY GAME
BE A TOURIST IN YOUR OWN TOWN FOR A DAY
TRY A NEW DISH AT YOUR FAVORITE RESTAURANT
TAKE A TRIP AND ONLY USE A DISPOSABLE CAMERA
THROW A SURPRISE PARTY
SING AT A KARAOKE NIGHT
RIDE A MECHANICAL BULL
HAVE A MOVIE MARATHON
VOLUNTEER AT A LOCAL CHARITY
WRITE EACH OTHER A LOVE LETTER

## BIG IDEAS

RIDE IN A HOT AIR BALLOON
TRAVEL TO A NEW COUNTRY
VISIT A NATIONAL PARK
GET MATCHING TATTOOS
GO ROCK CLIMBING
GO CAVE DIVING
GET MARRIED
LEARN TO SURF
BUY A HOUSE
START A BUSINESS TOGETHER
PICNIC SOMEWHERE UNEXPECTED
SEE ALL 7 WONDERS OF THE WORLD
SEE A BROADWAY SHOW
RIDE A TRAIN ACROSS CANADA
ADOPT A PET
GO SKYDIVING
BECOME A PARENT
TAKE A CRUISE
GO SCUBA DIVING
RUN A MARATHON TOGETHER
CLIMB A MOUNTAIN
VISIT A FOREIGN CITY
GO BUNGEE JUMPING

# SMALL BUCKET LIST IDEAS

# BIG BUCKET LIST IDEAS

# THE LIST

## WHERE DREAMS BECOME REALITY

Use the following pages to bring your life goals into
existence. Plan accordingly, and document the journey.

Don't forget to keep a form of proof, like a photograph or
ticket stub, from each adventure– otherwise no one will
believe you did it.

THE DREAM : _____

_____

DATE WRITTEN : _____ BIG GOAL : ☐ SMALL GOAL: ☐

WHY DO WE WANT TO DO THIS? : _____

_____

_____

_____

_____

## WHAT DO WE NEED TO DO TO ACCOMPLISH THIS?

| BABY STEPS | MAJOR STEPS |
|---|---|
| _____ | _____ |
| _____ | _____ |
| _____ | _____ |
| _____ | _____ |
| _____ | _____ |
| _____ | _____ |
| _____ | _____ |

DATE WE ACCOMPLISHED THE DREAM : _____

THE STORY : _____

_____

_____

_____

_____

_____

★ 01

WHAT WE LEARNED FROM THIS EXPERIENCE : _____

PROOF OF VICTORY :

THE DREAM : _____

_____

DATE WRITTEN : _____  BIG GOAL : ☐  SMALL GOAL: ☐

WHY DO WE WANT TO DO THIS? : _____

_____

_____

_____

_____

## WHAT DO WE NEED TO DO TO ACCOMPLISH THIS?

| BABY STEPS | MAJOR STEPS |
| --- | --- |

_____    _____

_____    _____

_____    _____

_____    _____

_____    _____

_____    _____

_____    _____

DATE WE ACCOMPLISHED THE DREAM : _____

THE STORY : _____

_____

_____

_____

_____

_____

_____

_____

_____

_____

_____

_____

_____

_____

**WHAT WE LEARNED FROM THIS EXPERIENCE :** _____

_____

_____

_____

_____

**PROOF OF VICTORY :**

THE DREAM : _____

_____

DATE WRITTEN : _____ BIG GOAL : ☐ SMALL GOAL: ☐

WHY DO WE WANT TO DO THIS? : _____

_____

_____

_____

_____

## WHAT DO WE NEED TO DO TO ACCOMPLISH THIS?

| BABY STEPS | MAJOR STEPS |
| --- | --- |
| _____ | _____ |
| _____ | _____ |
| _____ | _____ |
| _____ | _____ |
| _____ | _____ |
| _____ | _____ |
| _____ | _____ |

DATE WE ACCOMPLISHED THE DREAM : _____

THE STORY : _____

_____

_____

_____

_____

_____

_____

_____

_____

_____

_____

_____

_____

_____

_____

_____

**WHAT WE LEARNED FROM THIS EXPERIENCE :** _____

_____

_____

_____

**PROOF OF VICTORY :**

THE DREAM : _____

_____

DATE WRITTEN : _____ BIG GOAL : ☐ SMALL GOAL: ☐

WHY DO WE WANT TO DO THIS? : _____

_____

_____

_____

_____

## WHAT DO WE NEED TO DO TO ACCOMPLISH THIS?

| BABY STEPS | MAJOR STEPS |
| --- | --- |

_____    _____

_____    _____

_____    _____

_____    _____

_____    _____

_____    _____

_____    _____

DATE WE ACCOMPLISHED THE DREAM : _____

THE STORY : _____

_____

_____

_____

_____

_____

★ 04

_____
_____
_____
_____
_____
_____
_____
_____
_____

**WHAT WE LEARNED FROM THIS EXPERIENCE :** _____
_____
_____
_____
_____

**PROOF OF VICTORY :**

THE DREAM : _____

_____

DATE WRITTEN : _____  BIG GOAL : ☐  SMALL GOAL: ☐

WHY DO WE WANT TO DO THIS? : _____

_____

_____

_____

_____

## WHAT DO WE NEED TO DO TO ACCOMPLISH THIS?

| BABY STEPS | MAJOR STEPS |
|---|---|

DATE WE ACCOMPLISHED THE DREAM : _____

THE STORY : _____

_____

_____

_____

_____

_____

WHAT WE LEARNED FROM THIS EXPERIENCE : _____

PROOF OF VICTORY :

THE DREAM : _____

DATE WRITTEN : _____ BIG GOAL : ☐  SMALL GOAL: ☐

WHY DO WE WANT TO DO THIS? : _____

_____

_____

_____

_____

## WHAT DO WE NEED TO DO TO ACCOMPLISH THIS?

| BABY STEPS | MAJOR STEPS |
| --- | --- |

DATE WE ACCOMPLISHED THE DREAM : _____

THE STORY : _____

_____

_____

_____

_____

_____

_____

_____

_____

_____

_____

_____

_____

_____

_____

**WHAT WE LEARNED FROM THIS EXPERIENCE :** _____

_____

_____

_____

_____

**PROOF OF VICTORY :**

THE DREAM : _____

_____

DATE WRITTEN : _____  BIG GOAL : ☐  SMALL GOAL: ☐

WHY DO WE WANT TO DO THIS? : _____

_____

_____

_____

_____

## WHAT DO WE NEED TO DO TO ACCOMPLISH THIS?

| BABY STEPS | MAJOR STEPS |
|---|---|
| _____ | _____ |
| _____ | _____ |
| _____ | _____ |
| _____ | _____ |
| _____ | _____ |
| _____ | _____ |

DATE WE ACCOMPLISHED THE DREAM : _____

THE STORY : _____

_____

_____

_____

_____

_____

WHAT WE LEARNED FROM THIS EXPERIENCE :

PROOF OF VICTORY :

THE DREAM : _____

_____

DATE WRITTEN : _____ BIG GOAL : ☐ SMALL GOAL: ☐

WHY DO WE WANT TO DO THIS? : _____

_____

_____

_____

_____

## WHAT DO WE NEED TO DO TO ACCOMPLISH THIS?

| BABY STEPS | MAJOR STEPS |
|---|---|

_____     _____

_____     _____

_____     _____

_____     _____

_____     _____

_____     _____

_____     _____

DATE WE ACCOMPLISHED THE DREAM : _____

THE STORY : _____

_____

_____

_____

_____

_____

_____
_____
_____
_____
_____
_____
_____
_____
_____

**WHAT WE LEARNED FROM THIS EXPERIENCE :** _____

_____
_____
_____
_____

**PROOF OF VICTORY :**

THE DREAM : _____

_____

DATE WRITTEN : _____    BIG GOAL : ☐   SMALL GOAL: ☐

WHY DO WE WANT TO DO THIS? : _____

_____

_____

_____

_____

## WHAT DO WE NEED TO DO TO ACCOMPLISH THIS?

| BABY STEPS | MAJOR STEPS |
| --- | --- |

DATE WE ACCOMPLISHED THE DREAM : _____

THE STORY : _____

_____

_____

_____

_____

_____

★ 09

_____
_____
_____
_____
_____
_____
_____
_____
_____
_____

**WHAT WE LEARNED FROM THIS EXPERIENCE :** _____
_____
_____
_____

**PROOF OF VICTORY :**

THE DREAM : _____

DATE WRITTEN : _____ BIG GOAL : ☐ SMALL GOAL: ☐

WHY DO WE WANT TO DO THIS? : _____

_____

_____

_____

_____

## WHAT DO WE NEED TO DO TO ACCOMPLISH THIS?

| BABY STEPS | MAJOR STEPS |
|---|---|
| _____ | _____ |
| _____ | _____ |
| _____ | _____ |
| _____ | _____ |
| _____ | _____ |
| _____ | _____ |
| _____ | _____ |

DATE WE ACCOMPLISHED THE DREAM : _____

THE STORY : _____

_____

_____

_____

_____

_____

★ 10

WHAT WE LEARNED FROM THIS EXPERIENCE : _____

PROOF OF VICTORY :

THE DREAM : _____

_____

DATE WRITTEN : _____  BIG GOAL : ☐  SMALL GOAL: ☐

WHY DO WE WANT TO DO THIS? : _____

_____

_____

_____

_____

## WHAT DO WE NEED TO DO TO ACCOMPLISH THIS?

| BABY STEPS | MAJOR STEPS |
| --- | --- |

_____        _____

_____        _____

_____        _____

_____        _____

_____        _____

_____        _____

_____        _____

DATE WE ACCOMPLISHED THE DREAM : _____

THE STORY : _____

_____

_____

_____

_____

_____

_____

_____

_____

_____

_____

_____

_____

_____

_____

**WHAT WE LEARNED FROM THIS EXPERIENCE :** _____

_____

_____

_____

**PROOF OF VICTORY :**

THE DREAM : _____

_____

DATE WRITTEN : _____ BIG GOAL : ☐ SMALL GOAL: ☐

WHY DO WE WANT TO DO THIS? : _____

_____

_____

_____

_____

## WHAT DO WE NEED TO DO TO ACCOMPLISH THIS?

| BABY STEPS | MAJOR STEPS |
|---|---|
| _____ | _____ |
| _____ | _____ |
| _____ | _____ |
| _____ | _____ |
| _____ | _____ |
| _____ | _____ |
| _____ | _____ |

DATE WE ACCOMPLISHED THE DREAM : _____

THE STORY : _____

_____

_____

_____

_____

_____

_____
_____
_____
_____
_____
_____
_____
_____
_____
_____

**WHAT WE LEARNED FROM THIS EXPERIENCE :** _____
_____
_____
_____
_____

**PROOF OF VICTORY :**

THE DREAM : _____

_____

DATE WRITTEN : _____  BIG GOAL : ☐  SMALL GOAL: ☐

WHY DO WE WANT TO DO THIS? : _____

_____

_____

_____

_____

## WHAT DO WE NEED TO DO TO ACCOMPLISH THIS?

| BABY STEPS | MAJOR STEPS |
|---|---|

_____  _____

_____  _____

_____  _____

_____  _____

_____  _____

_____  _____

_____  _____

DATE WE ACCOMPLISHED THE DREAM : _____

THE STORY : _____

_____

_____

_____

_____

_____

_____

_____

_____

_____

_____

_____

_____

_____

_____

**WHAT WE LEARNED FROM THIS EXPERIENCE :** _____

_____

_____

_____

_____

**PROOF OF VICTORY :**

THE DREAM : _____

_____

DATE WRITTEN : _____  BIG GOAL : ☐  SMALL GOAL: ☐

WHY DO WE WANT TO DO THIS? : _____

_____

_____

_____

_____

## WHAT DO WE NEED TO DO TO ACCOMPLISH THIS?

| BABY STEPS | MAJOR STEPS |
| --- | --- |
| _____ | _____ |
| _____ | _____ |
| _____ | _____ |
| _____ | _____ |
| _____ | _____ |
| _____ | _____ |
| _____ | _____ |

DATE WE ACCOMPLISHED THE DREAM : _____

THE STORY : _____

_____

_____

_____

_____

_____

_____
_____
_____
_____
_____
_____
_____
_____
_____

**WHAT WE LEARNED FROM THIS EXPERIENCE :** _____
_____
_____
_____

**PROOF OF VICTORY :**

THE DREAM : _____

DATE WRITTEN : _____    BIG GOAL : ☐   SMALL GOAL: ☐

WHY DO WE WANT TO DO THIS? : _____

_____

_____

_____

_____

## WHAT DO WE NEED TO DO TO ACCOMPLISH THIS?

| BABY STEPS | MAJOR STEPS |
|---|---|
| _____ | _____ |
| _____ | _____ |
| _____ | _____ |
| _____ | _____ |
| _____ | _____ |
| _____ | _____ |

DATE WE ACCOMPLISHED THE DREAM : _____

THE STORY : _____

_____

_____

_____

_____

_____

_____

_____

_____

_____

_____

_____

_____

_____

_____

**WHAT WE LEARNED FROM THIS EXPERIENCE :** _____

_____

_____

_____

**PROOF OF VICTORY :**

THE DREAM : _____

_____

DATE WRITTEN : _____  BIG GOAL : ☐  SMALL GOAL: ☐

WHY DO WE WANT TO DO THIS? : _____

_____

_____

_____

_____

## WHAT DO WE NEED TO DO TO ACCOMPLISH THIS?

| BABY STEPS | MAJOR STEPS |
|---|---|

DATE WE ACCOMPLISHED THE DREAM : _____

THE STORY : _____

_____

_____

_____

_____

_____

_____

_____

_____

_____

_____

_____

_____

_____

_____

_____

**WHAT WE LEARNED FROM THIS EXPERIENCE :** _____

_____

_____

_____

_____

**PROOF OF VICTORY :**

THE DREAM : _____

DATE WRITTEN : _____ BIG GOAL : ☐ SMALL GOAL: ☐

WHY DO WE WANT TO DO THIS? : _____

_____

_____

_____

_____

## WHAT DO WE NEED TO DO TO ACCOMPLISH THIS?

| BABY STEPS | MAJOR STEPS |
|---|---|

DATE WE ACCOMPLISHED THE DREAM : _____

THE STORY : _____

_____

_____

_____

_____

_____

★ 17

_____
_____
_____
_____
_____
_____
_____
_____
_____

**WHAT WE LEARNED FROM THIS EXPERIENCE :** _____
_____
_____
_____
_____

**PROOF OF VICTORY :**

THE DREAM : _____

DATE WRITTEN : _____ BIG GOAL : ☐  SMALL GOAL: ☐

WHY DO WE WANT TO DO THIS? : _____

_____

_____

_____

_____

## WHAT DO WE NEED TO DO TO ACCOMPLISH THIS?

| BABY STEPS | MAJOR STEPS |
|------------|-------------|
| _____ | _____ |
| _____ | _____ |
| _____ | _____ |
| _____ | _____ |
| _____ | _____ |
| _____ | _____ |
| _____ | _____ |

DATE WE ACCOMPLISHED THE DREAM : _____

THE STORY : _____

_____

_____

_____

_____

_____

★ 18

_____

_____

_____

_____

_____

_____

_____

_____

_____

**WHAT WE LEARNED FROM THIS EXPERIENCE :** _____

_____

_____

_____

_____

**PROOF OF VICTORY :**

THE DREAM : _____

DATE WRITTEN : _____ BIG GOAL : ☐   SMALL GOAL: ☐

WHY DO WE WANT TO DO THIS? : _____

_____

_____

_____

_____

## WHAT DO WE NEED TO DO TO ACCOMPLISH THIS?

| BABY STEPS | MAJOR STEPS |
|---|---|

DATE WE ACCOMPLISHED THE DREAM : _____

THE STORY : _____

_____

_____

_____

_____

_____

_____
_____
_____
_____
_____
_____
_____
_____
_____
_____

**WHAT WE LEARNED FROM THIS EXPERIENCE :** _____
_____
_____
_____
_____

**PROOF OF VICTORY :**

THE DREAM : _____

_____

DATE WRITTEN : _____  BIG GOAL : [ ]  SMALL GOAL: [ ]

WHY DO WE WANT TO DO THIS? : _____

_____

_____

_____

_____

## WHAT DO WE NEED TO DO TO ACCOMPLISH THIS?

| BABY STEPS | MAJOR STEPS |
|---|---|

DATE WE ACCOMPLISHED THE DREAM : _____

THE STORY : _____

_____

_____

_____

_____

_____

★ 20

---
_____
_____
_____
_____
_____
_____
_____
_____
_____
_____

**WHAT WE LEARNED FROM THIS EXPERIENCE :** _____
_____
_____
_____
_____

**PROOF OF VICTORY :**

THE DREAM : _____

_____

DATE WRITTEN : _____ BIG GOAL : ☐ SMALL GOAL: ☐

WHY DO WE WANT TO DO THIS? : _____

_____

_____

_____

_____

## WHAT DO WE NEED TO DO TO ACCOMPLISH THIS?

| BABY STEPS | MAJOR STEPS |
|---|---|

DATE WE ACCOMPLISHED THE DREAM : _____

THE STORY : _____

_____

_____

_____

_____

_____

★ 21

---
---
---
---
---
---
---
---
---

**WHAT WE LEARNED FROM THIS EXPERIENCE :** _____

---
---
---
---

**PROOF OF VICTORY :**

THE DREAM : _____

_____

DATE WRITTEN : _____  BIG GOAL : ☐  SMALL GOAL: ☐

WHY DO WE WANT TO DO THIS? : _____

_____

_____

_____

_____

## WHAT DO WE NEED TO DO TO ACCOMPLISH THIS?

| BABY STEPS | MAJOR STEPS |
|---|---|

DATE WE ACCOMPLISHED THE DREAM : _____

THE STORY : _____

_____

_____

_____

_____

_____

WHAT WE LEARNED FROM THIS EXPERIENCE : _____

PROOF OF VICTORY :

THE DREAM : _____

_____

DATE WRITTEN : _____ BIG GOAL : ☐ SMALL GOAL: ☐

WHY DO WE WANT TO DO THIS? : _____

_____

_____

_____

_____

## WHAT DO WE NEED TO DO TO ACCOMPLISH THIS?

| BABY STEPS | MAJOR STEPS |
|---|---|

_____     _____

_____     _____

_____     _____

_____     _____

_____     _____

_____     _____

_____     _____

DATE WE ACCOMPLISHED THE DREAM : _____

THE STORY : _____

_____

_____

_____

_____

_____

_____

_____

_____

_____

_____

_____

_____

_____

_____

**WHAT WE LEARNED FROM THIS EXPERIENCE :** _____

_____

_____

_____

_____

**PROOF OF VICTORY :**

THE DREAM : _____

_____

DATE WRITTEN : _____   BIG GOAL : ☐   SMALL GOAL: ☐

WHY DO WE WANT TO DO THIS? : _____

_____

_____

_____

_____

## WHAT DO WE NEED TO DO TO ACCOMPLISH THIS?

| BABY STEPS | MAJOR STEPS |
| --- | --- |
| _____ | _____ |
| _____ | _____ |
| _____ | _____ |
| _____ | _____ |
| _____ | _____ |
| _____ | _____ |

DATE WE ACCOMPLISHED THE DREAM : _____

THE STORY : _____

_____

_____

_____

_____

_____

_____
_____
_____
_____
_____
_____
_____
_____
_____
_____

**WHAT WE LEARNED FROM THIS EXPERIENCE :** _____

_____
_____
_____
_____

**PROOF OF VICTORY :**

THE DREAM : _____

DATE WRITTEN : _____   BIG GOAL : ☐   SMALL GOAL: ☐

WHY DO WE WANT TO DO THIS? : _____

_____

_____

_____

_____

## WHAT DO WE NEED TO DO TO ACCOMPLISH THIS?

| BABY STEPS | MAJOR STEPS |
| --- | --- |

DATE WE ACCOMPLISHED THE DREAM : _____

THE STORY : _____

_____

_____

_____

_____

_____

_____

_____

_____

_____

_____

_____

_____

_____

**WHAT WE LEARNED FROM THIS EXPERIENCE :** _____

_____

_____

_____

**PROOF OF VICTORY :**

**26** ★

THE DREAM : _____

DATE WRITTEN : _____ BIG GOAL : ☐ SMALL GOAL: ☐

WHY DO WE WANT TO DO THIS? : _____

_____

_____

### WHAT DO WE NEED TO DO TO ACCOMPLISH THIS?

| BABY STEPS | MAJOR STEPS |
|---|---|

_____    _____

_____    _____

_____    _____

DATE WE ACCOMPLISHED THE DREAM : _____

THE STORY : _____

_____

_____

_____

_____

_____

_____

_____

WHAT WE LEARNED FROM THIS EXPERIENCE : _____

_____

_____

_____

★ 27

**THE DREAM :** _____

**DATE WRITTEN :** _____ **BIG GOAL :** ☐ **SMALL GOAL:** ☐

**WHY DO WE WANT TO DO THIS? :** _____
_____
_____

### WHAT DO WE NEED TO DO TO ACCOMPLISH THIS?

| BABY STEPS | MAJOR STEPS |
|---|---|

_____     _____
_____     _____
_____     _____

**DATE WE ACCOMPLISHED THE DREAM :** _____

**THE STORY :** _____
_____
_____
_____
_____
_____
_____
_____
_____

**WHAT WE LEARNED FROM THIS EXPERIENCE :** _____
_____
_____
_____

**28**

THE DREAM : _____

DATE WRITTEN : _____  BIG GOAL : ☐  SMALL GOAL: ☐

WHY DO WE WANT TO DO THIS? : _____

_____

_____

## WHAT DO WE NEED TO DO TO ACCOMPLISH THIS?

| BABY STEPS | MAJOR STEPS |
|---|---|

_____    _____

_____    _____

_____    _____

DATE WE ACCOMPLISHED THE DREAM : _____

THE STORY : _____

_____

_____

_____

_____

_____

_____

_____

_____

WHAT WE LEARNED FROM THIS EXPERIENCE : _____

_____

_____

_____

★ 29

THE DREAM : _____

DATE WRITTEN : _____  BIG GOAL : ☐  SMALL GOAL: ☐

WHY DO WE WANT TO DO THIS? : _____

_____

_____

## WHAT DO WE NEED TO DO TO ACCOMPLISH THIS?

| BABY STEPS | MAJOR STEPS |
|---|---|

DATE WE ACCOMPLISHED THE DREAM : _____

THE STORY : _____

_____

_____

_____

_____

_____

_____

_____

WHAT WE LEARNED FROM THIS EXPERIENCE : _____

_____

_____

_____

# 30 ★

THE DREAM : _____

DATE WRITTEN : _____ BIG GOAL : ☐ SMALL GOAL: ☐

WHY DO WE WANT TO DO THIS? : _____

_____

_____

## WHAT DO WE NEED TO DO TO ACCOMPLISH THIS?

| BABY STEPS | MAJOR STEPS |
|---|---|
| _____ | _____ |
| _____ | _____ |
| _____ | _____ |

DATE WE ACCOMPLISHED THE DREAM : _____

THE STORY : _____

_____

_____

_____

_____

_____

_____

_____

WHAT WE LEARNED FROM THIS EXPERIENCE : _____

_____

_____

_____

THE DREAM : _____

DATE WRITTEN : _____ BIG GOAL : ☐ SMALL GOAL: ☐

WHY DO WE WANT TO DO THIS? : _____

_____

_____

## WHAT DO WE NEED TO DO TO ACCOMPLISH THIS?

| BABY STEPS | MAJOR STEPS |
|---|---|

_____     _____

_____     _____

_____     _____

DATE WE ACCOMPLISHED THE DREAM : _____

THE STORY : _____

_____

_____

_____

_____

_____

_____

_____

WHAT WE LEARNED FROM THIS EXPERIENCE : _____

_____

_____

_____

**32** ★

THE DREAM : _____

DATE WRITTEN : _____ BIG GOAL : ☐  SMALL GOAL: ☐

WHY DO WE WANT TO DO THIS? : _____

_____

_____

### WHAT DO WE NEED TO DO TO ACCOMPLISH THIS?

| BABY STEPS | MAJOR STEPS |
|---|---|

_____  _____

_____  _____

_____  _____

DATE WE ACCOMPLISHED THE DREAM : _____

THE STORY : _____

_____

_____

_____

_____

_____

_____

_____

WHAT WE LEARNED FROM THIS EXPERIENCE : _____

_____

_____

_____

**THE DREAM :** _____

**DATE WRITTEN :** _____ **BIG GOAL :** ☐ **SMALL GOAL:** ☐

**WHY DO WE WANT TO DO THIS? :** _____

_____

_____

### WHAT DO WE NEED TO DO TO ACCOMPLISH THIS?

| BABY STEPS | MAJOR STEPS |
|---|---|

_____      _____

_____      _____

_____      _____

**DATE WE ACCOMPLISHED THE DREAM :** _____

**THE STORY :** _____

_____

_____

_____

_____

_____

_____

_____

_____

**WHAT WE LEARNED FROM THIS EXPERIENCE :** _____

_____

_____

_____

THE DREAM : _____

DATE WRITTEN : _____  BIG GOAL : ☐  SMALL GOAL: ☐

WHY DO WE WANT TO DO THIS? : _____

_____

_____

## WHAT DO WE NEED TO DO TO ACCOMPLISH THIS?

**BABY STEPS**

_____

_____

_____

**MAJOR STEPS**

_____

_____

_____

DATE WE ACCOMPLISHED THE DREAM : _____

THE STORY : _____

_____

_____

_____

_____

_____

_____

_____

_____

WHAT WE LEARNED FROM THIS EXPERIENCE : _____

_____

_____

_____

★ 35

THE DREAM : _____

DATE WRITTEN : _____  BIG GOAL : ☐  SMALL GOAL: ☐

WHY DO WE WANT TO DO THIS? : _____
_____
_____

## WHAT DO WE NEED TO DO TO ACCOMPLISH THIS?

| BABY STEPS | MAJOR STEPS |
|---|---|

_____  _____

_____  _____

_____  _____

DATE WE ACCOMPLISHED THE DREAM : _____

THE STORY : _____
_____
_____
_____
_____
_____
_____
_____

WHAT WE LEARNED FROM THIS EXPERIENCE : _____
_____
_____
_____

# 36 ★

THE DREAM : _____

DATE WRITTEN : _____ BIG GOAL : ☐ SMALL GOAL: ☐

WHY DO WE WANT TO DO THIS? : _____

_____

_____

## WHAT DO WE NEED TO DO TO ACCOMPLISH THIS?

| BABY STEPS | MAJOR STEPS |
|---|---|

DATE WE ACCOMPLISHED THE DREAM : _____

THE STORY : _____

_____

_____

_____

_____

_____

_____

_____

WHAT WE LEARNED FROM THIS EXPERIENCE : _____

_____

_____

_____

★ 37

THE DREAM : _____

DATE WRITTEN : _____  BIG GOAL : ☐  SMALL GOAL: ☐

WHY DO WE WANT TO DO THIS? : _____

_____

_____

## WHAT DO WE NEED TO DO TO ACCOMPLISH THIS?

| BABY STEPS | MAJOR STEPS |
|---|---|

_____      _____

_____      _____

_____      _____

DATE WE ACCOMPLISHED THE DREAM : _____

THE STORY : _____

_____

_____

_____

_____

_____

_____

_____

_____

WHAT WE LEARNED FROM THIS EXPERIENCE : _____

_____

_____

_____

**THE DREAM :** _____

**DATE WRITTEN :** _____  **BIG GOAL :** ☐  **SMALL GOAL:** ☐

**WHY DO WE WANT TO DO THIS? :** _____

_____

_____

## WHAT DO WE NEED TO DO TO ACCOMPLISH THIS?

| BABY STEPS | MAJOR STEPS |
|---|---|
| _____ | _____ |
| _____ | _____ |
| _____ | _____ |

**DATE WE ACCOMPLISHED THE DREAM :** _____

**THE STORY :** _____

_____

_____

_____

_____

_____

_____

**WHAT WE LEARNED FROM THIS EXPERIENCE :** _____

_____

_____

_____

★ 39

THE DREAM : _____

DATE WRITTEN : _____ BIG GOAL : ☐  SMALL GOAL: ☐

WHY DO WE WANT TO DO THIS? : _____

_____

_____

## WHAT DO WE NEED TO DO TO ACCOMPLISH THIS?

| BABY STEPS | MAJOR STEPS |
|---|---|

_____     _____

_____     _____

_____     _____

DATE WE ACCOMPLISHED THE DREAM : _____

THE STORY : _____

_____

_____

_____

_____

_____

_____

_____

_____

WHAT WE LEARNED FROM THIS EXPERIENCE : _____

_____

_____

_____

THE DREAM : _____

DATE WRITTEN : _____ BIG GOAL : ☐  SMALL GOAL: ☐

WHY DO WE WANT TO DO THIS? : _____

_____

_____

## WHAT DO WE NEED TO DO TO ACCOMPLISH THIS?

| BABY STEPS | MAJOR STEPS |
|---|---|

_____     _____

_____     _____

_____     _____

DATE WE ACCOMPLISHED THE DREAM : _____

THE STORY : _____

_____

_____

_____

_____

_____

_____

_____

WHAT WE LEARNED FROM THIS EXPERIENCE : _____

_____

_____

_____

★ 41

THE DREAM : _____

DATE WRITTEN : _____  BIG GOAL : ☐  SMALL GOAL: ☐

WHY DO WE WANT TO DO THIS? : _____

_____

_____

## WHAT DO WE NEED TO DO TO ACCOMPLISH THIS?

| BABY STEPS | MAJOR STEPS |

_____   _____

_____   _____

_____   _____

DATE WE ACCOMPLISHED THE DREAM : _____

THE STORY : _____

_____

_____

_____

_____

_____

_____

_____

WHAT WE LEARNED FROM THIS EXPERIENCE : _____

_____

_____

_____

**42**

THE DREAM : _____

DATE WRITTEN : _____  BIG GOAL : ☐  SMALL GOAL: ☐

WHY DO WE WANT TO DO THIS? : _____

_____

_____

## WHAT DO WE NEED TO DO TO ACCOMPLISH THIS?

| BABY STEPS | MAJOR STEPS |
|------------|-------------|
| _____ | _____ |
| _____ | _____ |
| _____ | _____ |

DATE WE ACCOMPLISHED THE DREAM : _____

THE STORY : _____

_____

_____

_____

_____

_____

_____

_____

WHAT WE LEARNED FROM THIS EXPERIENCE : _____

_____

_____

_____

★ 43

THE DREAM : _____

DATE WRITTEN : _____ BIG GOAL : ☐  SMALL GOAL: ☐

WHY DO WE WANT TO DO THIS? : _____

_____

_____

### WHAT DO WE NEED TO DO TO ACCOMPLISH THIS?

| BABY STEPS | MAJOR STEPS |
|---|---|

_____  _____

_____  _____

_____  _____

DATE WE ACCOMPLISHED THE DREAM : _____

THE STORY : _____

_____

_____

_____

_____

_____

_____

_____

WHAT WE LEARNED FROM THIS EXPERIENCE : _____

_____

_____

_____

**44**

THE DREAM : _____

DATE WRITTEN : _____ BIG GOAL : ☐ SMALL GOAL: ☐

WHY DO WE WANT TO DO THIS? : _____

_____

_____

## WHAT DO WE NEED TO DO TO ACCOMPLISH THIS?

| BABY STEPS | MAJOR STEPS |
|---|---|

_____   _____

_____   _____

_____   _____

DATE WE ACCOMPLISHED THE DREAM : _____

THE STORY : _____

_____

_____

_____

_____

_____

_____

_____

WHAT WE LEARNED FROM THIS EXPERIENCE : _____

_____

_____

_____

THE DREAM : _____

DATE WRITTEN : _____     BIG GOAL : ☐   SMALL GOAL: ☐

WHY DO WE WANT TO DO THIS? : _____

_____

_____

### WHAT DO WE NEED TO DO TO ACCOMPLISH THIS?

| BABY STEPS | MAJOR STEPS |
|---|---|

_____    _____

_____    _____

_____    _____

DATE WE ACCOMPLISHED THE DREAM : _____

THE STORY : _____

_____

_____

_____

_____

_____

_____

_____

_____

WHAT WE LEARNED FROM THIS EXPERIENCE : _____

_____

_____

_____

# 46 ★

THE DREAM : _____

DATE WRITTEN : _____  BIG GOAL : ☐  SMALL GOAL: ☐

WHY DO WE WANT TO DO THIS? : _____

_____

_____

## WHAT DO WE NEED TO DO TO ACCOMPLISH THIS?

| BABY STEPS | MAJOR STEPS |
|---|---|

_____  _____

_____  _____

_____  _____

DATE WE ACCOMPLISHED THE DREAM : _____

THE STORY : _____

_____

_____

_____

_____

_____

_____

_____

WHAT WE LEARNED FROM THIS EXPERIENCE : _____

_____

_____

_____

★ 47

THE DREAM : _____

DATE WRITTEN : _____    BIG GOAL : ☐   SMALL GOAL: ☐

WHY DO WE WANT TO DO THIS? : _____

_____

_____

## WHAT DO WE NEED TO DO TO ACCOMPLISH THIS?

| BABY STEPS | MAJOR STEPS |
|---|---|

_____    _____

_____    _____

_____    _____

DATE WE ACCOMPLISHED THE DREAM : _____

THE STORY : _____

_____

_____

_____

_____

_____

_____

_____

WHAT WE LEARNED FROM THIS EXPERIENCE : _____

_____

_____

_____

**48**

THE DREAM : _____

DATE WRITTEN : _____ BIG GOAL : ☐ SMALL GOAL: ☐

WHY DO WE WANT TO DO THIS? : _____

_____

_____

### WHAT DO WE NEED TO DO TO ACCOMPLISH THIS?

| BABY STEPS | MAJOR STEPS |
|------------|-------------|
| _____ | _____ |
| _____ | _____ |
| _____ | _____ |

DATE WE ACCOMPLISHED THE DREAM : _____

THE STORY : _____

_____

_____

_____

_____

_____

_____

_____

WHAT WE LEARNED FROM THIS EXPERIENCE : _____

_____

_____

_____

★ 49

**THE DREAM :** _____

**DATE WRITTEN :** _____  **BIG GOAL :** ☐  **SMALL GOAL:** ☐

**WHY DO WE WANT TO DO THIS? :** _____

_____

_____

### WHAT DO WE NEED TO DO TO ACCOMPLISH THIS?

| BABY STEPS | MAJOR STEPS |
|---|---|

_____     _____

_____     _____

_____     _____

**DATE WE ACCOMPLISHED THE DREAM :** _____

**THE STORY :** _____

_____

_____

_____

_____

_____

_____

_____

**WHAT WE LEARNED FROM THIS EXPERIENCE :** _____

_____

_____

_____

# 50

**THE DREAM :** _____

**DATE WRITTEN :** _____ **BIG GOAL :** ☐ **SMALL GOAL:** ☐

**WHY DO WE WANT TO DO THIS? :** _____

_____

_____

## WHAT DO WE NEED TO DO TO ACCOMPLISH THIS?

| BABY STEPS | MAJOR STEPS |
|---|---|
| _____ | _____ |
| _____ | _____ |
| _____ | _____ |

**DATE WE ACCOMPLISHED THE DREAM :** _____

**THE STORY :** _____

_____

_____

_____

_____

_____

_____

_____

**WHAT WE LEARNED FROM THIS EXPERIENCE :** _____

_____

_____

_____

★ 51

THE DREAM : _____

DATE WRITTEN : _____ BIG GOAL : ☐ SMALL GOAL: ☐

WHY DO WE WANT TO DO THIS? : _____

_____

_____

## WHAT DO WE NEED TO DO TO ACCOMPLISH THIS?

| BABY STEPS | MAJOR STEPS |
|------------|-------------|

_____     _____

_____     _____

_____     _____

DATE WE ACCOMPLISHED THE DREAM : _____

THE STORY : _____

_____

_____

_____

_____

_____

_____

_____

_____

WHAT WE LEARNED FROM THIS EXPERIENCE : _____

_____

_____

_____

# 52

THE DREAM : _____

DATE WRITTEN : _____ BIG GOAL : ☐ SMALL GOAL: ☐

WHY DO WE WANT TO DO THIS? : _____

_____

_____

## WHAT DO WE NEED TO DO TO ACCOMPLISH THIS?

| BABY STEPS | MAJOR STEPS |
|---|---|

_____  _____

_____  _____

_____  _____

DATE WE ACCOMPLISHED THE DREAM : _____

THE STORY : _____

_____

_____

_____

_____

_____

_____

_____

WHAT WE LEARNED FROM THIS EXPERIENCE : _____

_____

_____

_____

★ 53

THE DREAM : _____

DATE WRITTEN : _____  BIG GOAL : ☐  SMALL GOAL: ☐

WHY DO WE WANT TO DO THIS? : _____

_____

_____

### WHAT DO WE NEED TO DO TO ACCOMPLISH THIS?

| BABY STEPS | MAJOR STEPS |
|------------|-------------|
| _____ | _____ |
| _____ | _____ |
| _____ | _____ |

DATE WE ACCOMPLISHED THE DREAM : _____

THE STORY : _____

_____

_____

_____

_____

_____

_____

_____

WHAT WE LEARNED FROM THIS EXPERIENCE : _____

_____

_____

_____

**54** ★

THE DREAM : _____

DATE WRITTEN : _____ BIG GOAL : ☐ SMALL GOAL: ☐

WHY DO WE WANT TO DO THIS? : _____

_____

_____

### WHAT DO WE NEED TO DO TO ACCOMPLISH THIS?

| BABY STEPS | MAJOR STEPS |
|---|---|

_____     _____

_____     _____

_____     _____

DATE WE ACCOMPLISHED THE DREAM : _____

THE STORY : _____

_____

_____

_____

_____

_____

_____

_____

WHAT WE LEARNED FROM THIS EXPERIENCE : _____

_____

_____

_____

THE DREAM : _____

DATE WRITTEN : _____ BIG GOAL : ☐ SMALL GOAL: ☐

WHY DO WE WANT TO DO THIS? : _____
_____
_____

### WHAT DO WE NEED TO DO TO ACCOMPLISH THIS?

| BABY STEPS | MAJOR STEPS |
|---|---|

_____     _____

_____     _____

_____     _____

DATE WE ACCOMPLISHED THE DREAM : _____

THE STORY : _____
_____
_____
_____
_____
_____
_____
_____
_____

WHAT WE LEARNED FROM THIS EXPERIENCE : _____
_____
_____
_____

# 56

THE DREAM : _____

DATE WRITTEN : _____ BIG GOAL : ☐ SMALL GOAL: ☐

WHY DO WE WANT TO DO THIS? : _____

_____

_____

## WHAT DO WE NEED TO DO TO ACCOMPLISH THIS?

| BABY STEPS | MAJOR STEPS |
|---|---|

_____     _____

_____     _____

_____     _____

DATE WE ACCOMPLISHED THE DREAM : _____

THE STORY : _____

_____

_____

_____

_____

_____

_____

_____

_____

WHAT WE LEARNED FROM THIS EXPERIENCE : _____

_____

_____

_____

THE DREAM : _____

DATE WRITTEN : _____ BIG GOAL : ☐ SMALL GOAL: ☐

WHY DO WE WANT TO DO THIS? : _____

_____

_____

## WHAT DO WE NEED TO DO TO ACCOMPLISH THIS?

| BABY STEPS | MAJOR STEPS |
|---|---|
| _____ | _____ |
| _____ | _____ |
| _____ | _____ |

DATE WE ACCOMPLISHED THE DREAM : _____

THE STORY : _____

_____

_____

_____

_____

_____

_____

_____

WHAT WE LEARNED FROM THIS EXPERIENCE : _____

_____

_____

_____

## 58 ★

THE DREAM : _____

DATE WRITTEN : _____ BIG GOAL : ☐ SMALL GOAL: ☐

WHY DO WE WANT TO DO THIS? : _____

_____

_____

### WHAT DO WE NEED TO DO TO ACCOMPLISH THIS?

| BABY STEPS | MAJOR STEPS |
|---|---|
| _____ | _____ |
| _____ | _____ |
| _____ | _____ |

DATE WE ACCOMPLISHED THE DREAM : _____

THE STORY : _____

_____

_____

_____

_____

_____

_____

_____

WHAT WE LEARNED FROM THIS EXPERIENCE : _____

_____

_____

_____

★ 59

THE DREAM : _____

DATE WRITTEN : _____ BIG GOAL : ☐   SMALL GOAL: ☐

WHY DO WE WANT TO DO THIS? : _____

_____

_____

## WHAT DO WE NEED TO DO TO ACCOMPLISH THIS?

| BABY STEPS | | MAJOR STEPS |
|---|---|---|

_____     _____

_____     _____

_____     _____

DATE WE ACCOMPLISHED THE DREAM : _____

THE STORY : _____

_____

_____

_____

_____

_____

_____

_____

WHAT WE LEARNED FROM THIS EXPERIENCE : _____

_____

_____

_____

THE DREAM : _____

DATE WRITTEN : _____  BIG GOAL : ☐  SMALL GOAL: ☐

WHY DO WE WANT TO DO THIS? : _____

_____

_____

### WHAT DO WE NEED TO DO TO ACCOMPLISH THIS?

| BABY STEPS | MAJOR STEPS |
|---|---|

_____    _____

_____    _____

_____    _____

DATE WE ACCOMPLISHED THE DREAM : _____

THE STORY : _____

_____

_____

_____

_____

_____

_____

_____

WHAT WE LEARNED FROM THIS EXPERIENCE : _____

_____

_____

_____

**THE DREAM :** _____

**DATE WRITTEN :** _____  **BIG GOAL :** ☐  **SMALL GOAL:** ☐

**WHY DO WE WANT TO DO THIS? :** _____

_____

_____

## WHAT DO WE NEED TO DO TO ACCOMPLISH THIS?

| BABY STEPS | MAJOR STEPS |
|------------|-------------|
| _____ | _____ |
| _____ | _____ |
| _____ | _____ |

**DATE WE ACCOMPLISHED THE DREAM :** _____

**THE STORY :** _____

_____

_____

_____

_____

_____

_____

_____

_____

**WHAT WE LEARNED FROM THIS EXPERIENCE :** _____

_____

_____

_____

# PROOF

## PHOTO OR IT DIDN'T HAPPEN

It's true what they say... "photo or it didn't happen!" Use
this section of *Our Bucket List Adventures* to include photos
from your victories.

Tip: Photo stickers work great in this journal. You can have
your photos printed onto stickers through various online
printers, or, you can purchase a portable photo sticker
printer to use. It's not necessary by any means, but rather a
recommendation to consider.

# OUR BUCKET LIST INDEX

|  |  |
|---|---|
|  |  |
|  |  |
|  |  |
|  |  |
|  |  |
|  |  |
|  |  |
|  |  |
|  |  |
|  |  |
|  |  |
|  |  |
|  |  |
|  |  |
|  |  |
|  |  |
|  |  |
|  |  |
|  |  |
|  |  |
|  |  |
|  |  |
|  |  |
|  |  |
|  |  |

# OUR BUCKET LIST INDEX

|  |  |
|---|---|
|  |  |
|  |  |
|  |  |
|  |  |
|  |  |
|  |  |
|  |  |
|  |  |
|  |  |
|  |  |
|  |  |
|  |  |
|  |  |
|  |  |
|  |  |
|  |  |
|  |  |
|  |  |
|  |  |
|  |  |
|  |  |
|  |  |
|  |  |
|  |  |
|  |  |
|  |  |
|  |  |
|  |  |
|  |  |

# OUR BUCKET LIST INDEX

| | |
|---|---|
| | |
| | |
| | |
| | |
| | |
| | |
| | |
| | |
| | |
| | |
| | |
| | |
| | |
| | |
| | |
| | |
| | |
| | |
| | |
| | |
| | |
| | |
| | |
| | |

# EVERYONE HAS A STORY TO TELL

We firmly believe everyone has a story to tell, which is why we create the heirloom books that we do. We invite you to visit our website to dive into any of the books in our current lineup and get a deeper look at the contents, purpose of the book, who it's for, and what makes each one special.

**WWW.KORIEHEROLD.COM**